In All This Rain

IN ALL THIS RAIN

POEMS BY

John Stone

Louisiana State University Press
Baton Rouge and London 1980

Design: Patricia Douglas Crowder
Typeface: VIP Electra
Composition: LSU Press

Sixth printing (December, 1986)

Grateful acknowledgment is made to the following publications in which some of the poems first appeared: *American Scholar, Anlage, Annals of Internal Medicine, Bits, Briarcliff Press, Denver Quarterly, Greenhouse Review, Inlet, Journal of the Medical Association of Georgia, Midwest Quarterly, New England Review, New Orleans Review, New Virginia Review, New York Quarterly, Poetry Northwest, Raven, Sam Houston Literary Journal, Southern Poetry Review, Southern Poets.*

I am especially grateful to two people who helped me in the preparation of this manuscript: Mae Nelson, friend, listener, keeper of the nontemporal calendar; Miller Williams, friend, poet, consummate critic.

LIBRARY OF CONGRESS CATALOGING IN PUBLICATION DATA

Stone, John, 1936–
    In all this rain.

I. Title.
PS3569.T6413I5   811'.54   80–13762
ISBN 0–8071–0667–4
ISBN 0–8071–0668–2 (pbk.)

for Betsy
for Marler

genes, yes, but more

Contents

I THE MAN AT SECOND

The Words

having formed a more (nearly) perfect
union
are tired
have gathered around the fire
to say
no more
have had it
the words eat biscuits
and hyacinths
are tired
do not talk
want only to sleep
want rest beyond a semicolon;
have a headache
have a period
are not responsible for what
they do not say
have voted to quit
to strike
to abstain and refrain
have taken counsel together against the enemy
are no longer satisfied to be objects
direct or indirect

have for a half a year
made no graven images
just as it says in the Book
made a long time ago
when words were still working

but then you never could hire one cheap

He Makes a House Call

Six, seven years ago
when you began to begin to faint
I painted your leg with iodine

threaded the artery
with the needle and then the tube
pumped your heart with dye enough

to see the valve
almost closed with stone.
We were both under pressure.

Today, in your garden,
kneeling under the sticky fig tree
for tomatoes

I keep remembering your blood.
Seven, it was. I was just
beginning to learn the heart

inside out.
Afterward, your surgery
and the precise valve of steel

and plastic that still pops and clicks
inside like a ping-pong ball.
I should try

chewing tobacco sometimes
if only to see how it tastes.
There is a trace of it at the corner

of your leathery smile
which insists that I see inside
the house: someone named Bill I'm supposed

to know; the royal plastic soldier
whose body fills with whiskey
and marches on a music box

How Dry I Am;
the illuminated 3-D Christ who turns
into Mary from different angles;

the watery basement,
the pills you take, the ivy
that may grow around the ceiling

if it must. Here, you
are in charge—of figs, beans,
tomatoes, life.

At the hospital, a thousand times
I have heard your heart valve open, close.
I know how clumsy it is.

But health is whatever works
and for as long. I keep thinking
of seven years without a faint

on my way to the car
loaded with vegetables
I keep thinking of seven years ago

when you bled in my hands like a saint.

Love Poem at a Particular Breakfast
for No Particular Woman

This blueberry muffin
is on its way to becoming
your breast.
It is only part-way there,
not nearly far enough,
smaller, harder.

Nothing is perfect.
It is better so. Of course.

But it makes me want
to taste you.

I'd like, some muffin-morning,
to love you like the last movement
of Mozart's 22nd Piano Concerto.

But this blueberry muffin
at breakfast
is as good a place as any
to begin.

Brain

is
most like
a priest

who revels in
the body's feast

and says
too much
and asks
how long

and sings his own
electric song

until he totters
on his shelf
and as he falls
forgives himself.

Heart

The heart depends—
and learns too well
diastole
like any bell.
And systole
is what it sends.

And for its part
that's what it does:
it leaves the beat
the way it was
so that its end
becomes its start.

It dangles there
in perfect tone
repeats its prayer
for all its kin
behind the bone.
The heart thereby
survives all sin

except its own.

Losing a Voice in Summer

How many parts rumble it was
how much gravel
dark, light
I don't remember

and it won't echo for me
from the shower stall

though sometimes off the porch
calling my own sons for supper
I can almost

almost hear it

as if you had let it go
out of the corner
of your mouth
like a ventriloquist
without a dummy.

I have no recording

otherwise I would play you
in the shower, repeat you
off the porch

from the cat-walk
of the glass factory have you sing
Go Down Moses
over and over and

tonight
with the reluctant sentence
deep in my head at the hoarsest hour,
dumb and laryngitic and alone

I first understood
how completely I have lost your voice,
father, along with my own.

9

Death

I have seen   come on
slowly as rust
sand

or suddenly   as when
someone leaving
a room

finds the doorknob
come loose in his hand

Parable

. . . for it is better to marry than to burn.
I CORINTHIANS 7:9

He's the sullen, mulling sort,
happy as the day is short.

She's the apple of his eye;
add some sugar, she's a pie.

              *

After church, sometimes before,
they drove, parked in a puff of dirt,

And Mary showed Tom a little more
religious freedom under her skirt.

              *

Tom and Mary now have found
a married sort of middle ground,

something they had both dreamed of
longer than lust, shorter than love.

              *

Rejecting this one, weighing that,
they've considered all the factors.

If now her love has turned to fat,
if all he thinks about is tractors,

still even slow souls do embrace
and growing old with time, not grace,

each in the mirror finds the other's face.

Room 2405

If I am very quiet

I can hear
the ice machine
making itself turn on

I have the feeling
that no one else
is on this floor

I am a convention
called and met
by myself

addressing myself
to you
a thousand miles away

Now
I am addressing
myself

If
as they say
everything done

is done out of revenge
or love
or fear of dying

you know which one

this is

Dreaming Awake

Lying, watching the storm
run out of lightning

with the thunder scaring off
in the distance

I am mainly eyes and ears.

In the grog minutes
before sleep

I can see my dead father's face
made up of dots and light
as though seen through
the back screen door

through which he comes now
wet to the eyebrows
but smiling home
for supper

and bringing
the whole dangerous outdoors

inside with him

tamed and joyful.

The Truck

I was coming back from
wherever I'd been when
I saw the truck and
the sign on the back repeated
on the side to be certain
you knew it was no mistake

PROGRESS CASKETS

ARTHUR ILLINOIS

Now folks have different
thoughts it's true about
death but in general it's
not like any race for
example you ever ran
everyone wanting to come in

last and all   And I admit
a business has to have a good
name   No one knows better
than I the value of a good
name   A name is what sells
the product in the first

and in the final place
All this time the Interstate
was leading me into Atlanta
and I was following the sign
and the truck was heavier
climbing the hill than

going down which is as
it should be   What I really
wanted to see was the driver
up close maybe talk to him
find out his usual run
so I could keep off it

Not that I'm superstitious   It's just
the way I was raised   A casket
may be Progress up in Arthur
but it's thought of
down here
as a setback.

NOEL: A Christmas Poem

I walk the cold dark
of my backyard

where the tops of the pines
still try for stars.

Inside, my sons sleep
in dreams the shapes
of footballs and feathers.
They have not been told
how fast we are all dying.

I think of the cattle
urine rising like steam
in the barn at Bethlehem,
the Boy crying.

I pee for joy.

Poem in Praise of Perfect Pants

Inspected by No. 9.
In case of defect, return
this tag with garment.

Number 9,
I found your tag in the pocket.
The pants fit, a fact
not altogether your doing
since I have just readjusted
my own inches.

Still, at the other end
of whatever belt loop,
I imagine you—
a woman, a wife,

someone's mother,
with too many kinds of inspections
to make already. Someone else
will have to be grateful for those.

But I thank you
for these perfect pants.

I will keep the tag as a charm
against all future irregulars

which may have been inspected
and sent away
without love.

That, of course, is the only
unredeemable defect.

Love Poem Entirely of Clichés

Breathing a word
but strictly between us

there is this about you

on the one hand
or the other

on the tip of my tongue.

You of all things
and of all people.

The Parable of the Instruments

And one man they took
    off to the side and said to him
    you are a welder and put
    in his hands an acetylene torch
    which he afterward took
    everywhere with him aflame
    spurting blue fire and hissing
    and he became in his own time
    an expert

Another in the crowd
    they sidled up to and said
    this is a gun which makes you
    of course
    a soldier and his trigger finger
    itched from that day backward

But the man with his tongue
    loose congenitally at both ends
    needed no other instruments
    He spoke out of both sides
    of his mouth   He threw
    his voice over there and over
    there and it came back to him
    like a boomerang

They offered me   on the quietus
    a calendar/date book combination
    a lock to pick
    a pair of telephone-pole-climbing
        boots
    test tubes
    a vacuum cleaner
    the chance to be first in the parade
    a white horse to ride
    a black horse

I said no thanks

    but that man over there   I said
    throwing those words around
    do you think he could spare
    maybe
    a brand-new preposition or an adverb?

They said they'd ask him

I haven't heard a thing since January

Anatomy Lecture: The Female Pelvis

The vagina is a potential space.

We took notes with serious face
and tried to learn, not memorize,
all she taught with professional grace.

But it took years to realize
what she said about such space:
potential, impossible, or otherwise.

The Man

standing at attention
in his driveway
ignores his children's pleas

to come in, stands all day
in his driveway like a door
expecting keys

will not come in
for supper, will not even
say what he sees

straight ahead over the neighbor's
lawn, has been used by dogs,
is wet to the knees

is simply waiting to be told
by the Sergeant
wherever he is

at ease

Double-Header

Each and every one of us has got a schedule to keep.
—a truck driver being interviewed on radio

I've made it
have been left alone in the stadium
locked here after the baseball
twilight game, having hidden
where I won't tell

on a bet with someone I invented
and therefore had to win.
I can hear the Security Guard
locking up, watch him making his way out,
turning off the lights as he goes

toward home and supper, away from
the smell of popcorn and beer.
I can see him look
with a question at my car,
the only one besides his

still in the lot and see him
look back once at the stadium without
knowing or even thinking I could be
looking back at him, my face barbed
with wire. I turn now to the stadium

that is all mine, bought
with my money, purchased with
a three dollar ticket for the top tier,
the stadium that is coming alive again
with the crowd that is coming back

but of course isn't coming back
to watch me play, with DiMaggio in center,
Cobb in left, Hornsby at second
Rizzuto at short, and all the others
who have been tagged out more than once

themselves, and who will get me later
or sooner, trying to stretch a single
into a double, catching up with my lost breath
that I can remember now from when
I was eleven, with a stitch in my side

sprinting still in spite of the stitch
for the inside-the-park home run
I almost had when I was twelve
for the girl I almost got when I got
old enough but didn't know the rules

dusting my pants off now
to the music I never learned, for
the symphony orchestra I never conducted,
my hands rough with rosin
for the truck I never drove

and the fish I never caught
and wouldn't have known if I had
how to take him off the hook,
for my father who is in the crowd
cheering out his heart

but who of course isn't there
as I pull up lame at second
with a stand-up double
in this game that goes on for hours,
my hands stinging with the bat,

the All-Stars aligned against me
in this stadium I own for the night,
one great circle and inside this circle
this square that seems the only one
on this curving darkening ball of earth

or the only one anyway
marked by bases I must run all night
for everything I should
by now
be worth.

In All This Rain

for Doktor Bruder,
the dachshund

Despite
what is written
about the rain

love is the one element
that takes more sense
than any other

to know when
to come in out of.
It rains

sooner or later of course on
everything we bury
And burying a dog

is not
according to the experts
supposed to be anything like

as painful
as burying your kin.
They say

think of it as a sleep
in which the stars also
all go out at once

the stars that you know
are still up there
but just can't see.

I stopped
a long time ago trying
to make sense

out of all this business
of giving up the ghost.
I find no consolation

in this brown fact
of your dying
which reminds me only

that no man
is any deader
than his dog.

I don't believe
you're better off.
Those of us looking up

can still see the stars
at least when it's
not raining. We've kept

the box
of a house where you lived
49 years of a dog's life.

I'd like you to know
that when I told Jim,
"Dok's gone,"

he said,
"You mean he's dead."
And went over to the couch

where you used to sprawl.
And cried.
Later he said,

"Next dog
I want one that lasts."

II THE SELF-CONTAINED WOMAN

A Cliché Poem for Your Leaving

Last things first.
I would not by the hair of my chin
utter a word against you
except to ask where in hell
is the silver lining.

No news is not necessarily

says the philosopher, pleased
with himself, his head buried,
and as always, just enough off
the mark of the real world
to appear as wise as he is old.

I hope to God

I don't pass this way again.
As it is the best place to end
was at the beginning
as it were.
For the time being

holding the short end of the stick

I mean to contemplate
only until six of one
seems once more
half a dozen.
I am well, also alive.

It's just a matter of time
until the truth
will out.
Till then, I am resigned
in name only and, as before
left to my own devices.

Epithalamium Beginning with the Letter W

W is for the wedding
of this woman and this man

Let your twoness be as one
as much as twoness can

though let your one be also two.
And let the letter W stand

for all it came from to:
may you begin, as it began,

a double you.

for Betsy and Knox

Starting Over

When I got here

there were only the coal belts
stretched around the belly
of the world

and you, off in one corner
of the garden, by some
spontaneous fire

learning the functions
of the thumb over
slowly and over

What I didn't know then

was how much there would be
to discard
after such a short time:

the apple core
of course
and there were more than one

the markings on the cave
to be erased
the children

And the everlasting
angel feathers at the gate

I'll take the responsibility
if you'll take the blame

Whittling: The Last Class

What has been written
about whittling
is not true

most of it

It is the discovery
that keeps
the fingers moving

not idleness

but the knife looking for
the right plane
that will let the secret out

Whittling is no pastime

he says
who has been whittling
in spare minutes at the wood

of his life for forty years

Three rules he thinks
have helped
Make small cuts

In this way

you may be able to stop before
what was to be an arm
has to be something else

Always whittle away from yourself

and toward something.
For God's sake
and your own

know when to stop

Whittling is the best example
I know of what most
may happen when

least expected

bad or good
Hurry before
angina comes like a pair of pliers

over your left shoulder

There is plenty of wood
for everyone
and you

Go ahead now

May you find
in the waiting wood
rough   unspoken

what is true

or
nearly true
or

true enough.

Where There Is a Hospital

there is a child
to be sick in it
and where there is a child

there is a mother
But the child.
Who gives up his blood

to be examined
and is still a child
who must have X-rays

antibiotics
shining instruments
clean as the inside

of an eye. The child
receiving disease
as a tree its shadow.

                    *

Is this child my child
is this child I when I
was a child is this

the child I will be
The child sits like a Buddha
with all the answers

if only he would say them.

The Good Bait Wiggles

What the upper lip knows
the lower will learn.

*

In thirty years of sinful living
I've found no sin worth its forgiving.

*

Because is reason enough till why.

*

Certainty is a dead donkey
that doesn't know it yet.

*

Only the deaf and nearly dead can know
how far back in the head the tongue can go.

*

Dr. Stone is indisposed;
that is why his door is closed.

*

This is a dawn I could wake to, but don't—
to balance the one I should wake to, and won't.

*

I am standing in front of the Xerox machine
singing Bach in its honor.

*

Though some other be your ghost
I will haunt you more than most.

*

The good bait wiggles
at the right time.

*

One last thing before I hang up: Hello.

Poem on Momentous Themes After
e. e. cummings

John is my name
which is as good as any

and better than some
It is spring now in this

year of our Lord. The trees, though
and the flowers are nothing

next to the human sap
that is rising

next to the girls
in cut-offs

next to their navels which
have been covered since the Fall

next to the eternal spring
of a woman's bottom

which makes me
as she passes

wonder how and why it is
gravity reaches up

and grabs us all
finally by the

ask any question you like
the answer is the same

Death, what's more,
never forgets a name.

Mr. G.

No one should die in 1967 of a dead battery. So when I first saw
Mr. G. with his heart rate of 30 a minute, I knew he needed a
pacemaker: a new battery for his heart which missed the 70 beats a
minute it was supposed to get. Otherwise, he was in good 64-year-
old shape.

It did take some talking, though. The Bible says don't mess
around with things too much; His eye is on the sparrow; the hairs
on your head are numbered. That sort of thing. So I told him the
truth, but as Emily Dickinson said to do, I told it "slant," only
mentioning the dire consequences of *not* having a pacemaker,
such as stroke, heart attack, falling out spells, broken hip or head.

And I told him sometimes the doctor has to help God.

He consented, after a couple of perilous nights at a rate of 30, to
a temporary pacemaker—a wire threaded along an arm vein into
the heart and pulsed by an external battery. He immediately felt
better. Two weeks later he allowed us to put in a permanent
pacemaker, this time the battery surgically placed in a small
pouch in the abdomen. And Mr. G. felt great.

Eight years passed and several batteries were changed, a simple
surgical procedure done every two or three years under local
anesthesia. He continued to feel fine, the clock under his belt
blipping its 70 times a minute with immaculate regularity.
Periodically, he dropped by the office for my reassuring check
of his pulse at the wrist. Most of the time he checked it himself,
twice a day, at home, testing its rate by holding a radio over his
abdomen and listening for the sharp merciful static the battery
makes. At first he was almost as afraid of the battery as he was
dependent on it. But he got used to it with time.

Two years ago, he came to the office in mid-dead-winter with an outsized coat and no sweater, but smiling. I told him he needed a sweater and I'd bring him one of mine from home, a woolly warm one my mother had given me that didn't match a thing I'd gotten any Christmas. He was to come back for it in a few days.

He didn't come back.

Outside the office window the seasons passed, several of them, and no Mr. G. By the next winter I'd given up on him. The body is heir to many problems besides battery problems. I wrote a poem about him. I took the sweater home.

Yesterday, ten years after his first battery, he smiled in through the doorway to the office. I was astonished and my face showed it. "I thought you'd—*moved*, Mr. G."

"You thought I was dead," he said. "You thought I was dead."

The Girl in the Hall

with the Mickey Mouse
watch tells me the time

without knowing

that I have come up
the stairs
from a crushed leg
scared eyes

and the stump
blood   bandages

the bones of the stretcher

he is gradually getting used to

the fact of no leg
below the knee
no toes to wiggle
though they move still
in his mind's foot

which remembers now only
the crane coming down on it.

She glances at her wrist.

In his head's watch
in the middle of morphine
he clutches the giant hands
like Harold Lloyd holding on
at half past five
while the cars line up
below him.

The expressway roars outside.

She asks.
I say I'm fine.

She has her clocks.
He, his.
I, mine.

Epitaphs

The Auctioneer
Just before the Coffin-Lidder
nails the eternal ceiling on,
tell the next-to-the-highest bidder
I am going, going, gone.

The Magician
I pulled a rabbit from my hat,
rejoined the severed ends of flannel;
I left them guessing at all that
then stepped into this secret panel.

La Grande Dame
People would tell me what they'd heard.
I thought their prophecy would miss.
I'd been taught that, in a word,
I was better than all this.

The Writer
Let the devil play the zither.
Let the angels play their harps.
Given choice, I'd rather
leave a corpus than a corpse.

The Weaver
When Clotho says
you're out of thread,
that's not what she means.
She means you're dead.

The Self-Contained Woman

As God is my witness, I was reading the life of Emily Dickinson when the woman shuffled in through the door of The Jumping Jack. The Jack is a literal hole-in-the-wall, but serves good omelettes, one of which I was eating when she came in out of the Chicago wind. She immediately claimed one of the tables, deposited her belongings on it, and ordered breakfast as if there were no one but her and the waitress in the restaurant.

She was fiftyish, with oil-gray hair that looked like a poorly fitting wig. She brought her meager breakfast back to her table and set about her business, which, it turned out, was considerable.

Her business was contained in two large plastic shopping bags, each of which displayed on top of the contents a large coat—both were imitation leather and heavy, though it was May and 75 degrees outside. She removed the coats, draped them over a chair-back, and began to methodically spread out over the whole table the contents of the plastic bags. During the next hour or so, while I sat and watched, ready to dip into my book if she threatened to look at me, she appeared oblivious to all that went on around her. People came in carrying everything from bicycle wheels to art canvases and ordering breakfast, but she was completely absorbed.

From the bags she took packet after packet of photographs, neatly held together with rubber bands; and a Polaroid camera which she placed carefully on the table, so that it aimed straight at me. Then she pulled out a purse, a wallet, a pocket album containing still more pictures. A large red shawl. A letter opener. Stacks of old letters, also bound with rubber bands. And brochures from several Chicago hotels, bound with a large paper clip.

She shuffled and re-sorted the pictures, according to some private order. Periodically she propped up one of the pictures on the unfolded bellows of the camera. One was a wedding scene, bride and groom; others were family-type snapshots. In the middle of all this, there were pictures of Chicago skyscrapers and other city landmarks. And last, publicity shots of Alan Ladd and William Bendix, clearly from an old movie advertisement.

It was as if she had brought her life with her to this place and spread it out on that table. I tried to turn my attention to my book. I thought of Emily in Amherst; and of the packets of poems neatly tied together and found by her family after her death. Almost an hour had passed. I was on my third cup of coffee. And the same page.

Finally, she gradually gathered up her things and replaced them in the bags, threw the shawl around her shoulders, and clomped toward the door. The things that mattered seemed to be, for the moment, in order. I followed her out the door of The Jack and watched as she trundled off into the bright Chicago sun, a sack in each arm, perfectly balanced and making, as she went, her own good sense.

Helping With the Math Homework

In the beginning
there were polynomials

differences of squares
trial and error

and the sum of two cubes.
X^2 minus Y^2

has always had
the same meaning

whatever it is.
But when Pythagoras

looked into
the eye of the triangle

and saw the solution
I wasn't there.

Nor have I ever found
anything more

than safety in numbers.
This is the new math

these are your problems
and I was born

before the back of the book.
What I have been saying is this:

I can lead you
only so far into wisdom.

Soon
you must begin to learn

how to be ignorant
on your own.

Death of a Comedian

Today, lowering you,
we were reminded

that

no matter how the story
is told, the end is not funny

that

the audience will
go on laughing anyway

that

the language has more words
for sadness than for joy

that

it is a serious matter
when a man tires

of his own jokes.

III NOW
WHAT

Attention

If you need an example
to hold your attention
say *these* hands and arms

or some just like them
these hands and arms anyway
for our purposes

are stretched out in the air

waiting

One of the marks
says the wise man
letting his attention stray

of getting older
is your attention span
gets longer up at least

to a point
but I maintain
it's not your span gets longer

it's you have
more to see
closer

And you think
you understand why the hands
and arms are stretched out

why the hands are there
waiting
you think you understand it all

then a football comes by
and the hands miss it

and you realize you didn't
understand at all
what the hands were waiting for

but you want to see it again
so you wait
your hands folded in your lap

but they don't show it again

or if they do you are asleep
which is just as well
because

this time
it was a running play
up the middle

But maybe after all
you were supposed to be watching
something other than the hands

for all this time
for all this investment of
your eyes

And what was the rest of you
doing
while your eyes

thought
they had it all figured out?
Not, I'll bet, paying attention.

Answering the Phone

Used to
you'd say
Hello
and think nothing of it

or someone else might do it
for you
He's out may I take a message
and you'd return the call

When Bobby died
and the man across the street
and Bill
and Mr. G.

all that changed
and you think
now before you answer the phone
you take a deep breath

and think something of it
and you know
no one else can ever answer
for you again

so now you pick up the receiver
and say not hello but
now what

now what

Lessons in the Subjunctive

That the door be opened
    the knob whispers
    to the hinges

That the child be found
    the grass is bent
    in the direction
    of his sleeping

That the midnight come
    the clock admits
    its only habit

That there be some kind of answer
    the tongue lies in its teeth

That the war be over
    the war is over

That the violin play
    the fingers leap and glide

That the string may say

That the bow decide

One Evening

And he said *for God's sake*
looking Death in the kisser

they said *how much insulin*
water
how much digitalis

and he said *I need a drink*
and he didn't mean water

they said *the rules don't*
allow it
about the time

Hutchins was catching
the long pass on the three

yard line and tripping
forward for the touchdown
about the time

the father was saying
go to sleep and I don't mean

maybe half the world
was standing on their heads
and didn't give an

anyway the sun came up
the time was recorded and copies

made about the time
all 14 billion milliequivalents
of him said in a loud barely but

audible voice
to hell with this

Looking Down into a Ditch

Watching the workmen dig a ditch
watching them lay in the pipe

for the waste and gasses
and liquids of our living

I think of the lost maps
of lost cities, their pipes
still moving off
in important directions

of people I knew
who are now in the serious dirt

of the ditches at Dachau

of my father.

It is hard
to keep remembering
across the ditches we have made
and covered over
with terrible earth-moving sound

how much of our dying
we must find ways not to need,
how much of what keeps us alive
is underground.

Fugue

*. . . the most highly developed
form of contrapuntal imitation
based on the principle of the
equality of the parts.*

This, dear, is *presto*
    and this *sostenuto*
Now for *glissando*
    a sliding of winds

A slight *ritardando*
    is all I can manage
such *appassionato*
    the music portends

We've tried it *con brio*
    bolero, calmato
a tempo, crescendo
    (The curtain descends)

You are the *alto*
    to my *basso buffo*
The score says *legato*
    The tempo depends

on the mood of the maestro
    And now *furioso*
amaro, sforzando!
    With what *accordando*

this symphony ends.

Causes

What do they do first?
*They examine the body
to prove that death
was natural.*

And if not?
Further tests.

And if natural?
*No one is ever
completely sure.*

But what of the family?
*They know, but are
not talking.*

And after all are satisfied?
All are never satisfied.

And what of those who are not?
*They are watched closely
to see if their deaths
are natural.*

And if not?
Further tests.

And So

another evening full of her
his mouth rekissed
with believable lies

arm, hand bones turn, twist
he paints the ceiling with his eyes
and love moves down along his wrist.

After Love

which is what
she has not been making
there will be time for thought
about keeping and taking

for recalling, one night older,
all she was told to fear:
same lunging shoulder
and breathing in her ear.

Progressions

1

touch wood for luck
touch skin for love
touch both for what
I'm thinking of.

2

O.K., Lucasta,
send me off to the wars.

Go get 'em, baby.

3

mouth   hands   thighs   bed
cane   crutches   wheelchair

dead

4

Born stiff
Lived stiff
Died (of course)
Stiff.

Emergency Power: 5 A.M.

Electrons slow and stop,
clogging the wires.
For 60 seconds, blood is not red,
bone not white—
the hospital is dark
as the inside of a heart.

For this long minute
we have all gone blind.

Then the partial light
of diesels:

On the tenth floor
in emergency power
a baby is born in its own time.

And now a light
another
a row of lights.

I come back to my desk
that was always there,
flick on the overhead lights
that were out without even knowing it.

I go upstairs
to speak to the new-born:
he answers me with his babiest cry,
having just come out of his own darkness

having passed the test with us all
here in the bloom of the hospital
with new breath coming out of the walls
and every clock but his
ten minutes slow forever.

Bringing Her Home

While you were in the hospital
the house was sick as hell.

I should have said the children
are well. And the turtles.

The kettle was cured with singing.

But your dresses
were breathless in the closet.
And then the demented washer
began to knock while spinning;
the dryer died wet as diapers.
And in one seizure of wind
the hinges on the doors
got palsy.

All last night
I was afraid of mushrooms.

No matter now.
The children and the turtles
are waiting for you there.
They are well.

But the close-mouthed keyholes and I
have been gasping for air.

He Takes the Course in Advanced Cardiac Life Support

Some patients who have been resuscitated request
that they not be rescued should they die again.

Kneeling over the dummy
giving her mouth to mouth
his breath

he presses her ample chest
80 times a minute
giving her the life

she never asked for
but keeps demanding
on the paper that unrolls

from her side like a ticker tape
A tracing that looks like life
is what is required

to pass this test
He cannot help but think
while he bends and pumps

above her one-*and*, two-*and*
three *et cetera*
of the little death

Finally sweating and
for lack of breath and help
he has to let her die

Which she promptly does
and the paper stops unwinding
As he tries to get up

he finds his left leg
has gone to sleep
And for a moment

he cannot move it
cannot move
caught between

the electricity coming out of
and the pain flowing into
the leg

He thinks
big death may be like this
like his left leg

gone to sleep
trying to stay alive
but tired

hurting just right
and barely enough
so you don't know

which is better
to wake back up
or to die

and you want it to stop
and you don't
but it does

or it doesn't

Building the Steps

She said to me
after I had already started
at the top

always start at the bottom
and I believed her
but as I say

I had already started
and at that
at the top

She had that look
on her face
one has to believe

She will be
when I finish
surely at the bottom

As I place the last stone
she must be first
to try them out

Up they must go and down
equally well
for either of us

like the road to town
like the bones of my back
hoping the last step

is where her foot
would have it
up as she wants it now

or down

Lament for the End of the Year

Why this singing, Brother John,
slow and early, before noon?
And why so clearly out of tune?
I sing for this year, nearly gone.

Out of Sunday's lack of grace
I mourn the older younger sons
who still reload and fire the guns.
I sing for what will not erase

despite the washings of monsoon;
for the country's long malaise
that cracked the world and lets it craze.
I sing because the heart's immune;

because this day begins the week
that starts the month that ends the year
in which I learned how not to hear.
I sing because I cannot speak.

In Praise of Even Plastic

And doubt all else. But praise.
—JOHN CIARDI

Praise, for one thing, this flower
that knew better than to be a flower
and grew plastic leaves and stem.

Praise my lost tooth, now replaced
and chewing better.
Praise this nerveless tooth.

Praise also the dreams I remember
good or bad.
The counterfeiter under the naked bulb

the con man
for what fools us where we live.
Praise the woman

who isn't sure
for what she is sure of.
The music in the grooves

all perpetual motion machines
lifetime guarantees.
Praise the plastic then

and dacron and fiber glass
as some hope against decay.
Praise the falseness that is true.

Praise the lie that lasts.

Even Though

A = pi r squared

even if a body
continues to fall
32 feet per second per second

which I hope

it will continue to do
nevertheless
after careful calculation

and by the grace of algebra

I am persuaded that
if truth is a number
not only is it never

in the back of the book

but it never comes out even
ends in a fraction
cannot be rounded off.

Approximation
was the first art.
It is the only science.

How I'd Have It

I'd have no flowers
other than Mozart

A suit—blue—
not new, but worn

the knees
still in the trousers

for as long
as polyester is

And a fire
and someone there

to throw on
the oak especially

for the last movement
of the Mozart

As for the mourners
let's have them enter

STAGE LEFT
and pause and peer

over the side
and say mournful

things such as What
A Pity A Pity

And So Old, Too.
And then exit all

STAGE RIGHT

A Nature Poem Written Indoors

Consider

the tadpole
on its slimy way
toward hop

the bear in its deepest
sleep but one

the butterfly
breaking out its wings

and you and I
having switched
through bird from fish
to this

to hair from fur.

Little keeps us as we are.
We survive by what we were.